THE *Skinny*
HOT AIR FRYER
COOKBOOK

D0957811

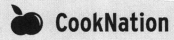 CookNation

The Skinny Hot Air Fryer Cookbook
Delicious & Simple Meals For Your Hot Air Fryer:
Discover the Healthier Way To Fry.

A Bell & Mackenzie Publication
First published in 2014 by Bell & Mackenzie Publishing
Limited.
Copyright © Bell & Mackenzie Publishing 2014

ISBN 978-1-909855-47-2

A CIP catalogue record of this book is available from the
British Library

Disclaimer
This book is designed to provide information on the dishes
that can be cooked in an electric Hot Air Frying appliance.
However all devices vary so please ensure you follow the
cooking guidelines and instructions for your individual
device.
Some recipes may contain nuts or traces of nuts. Those
suffering from any allergies associated with nuts should
avoid any recipes containing nuts or nut based oils.
This information is provided and sold with the knowledge
that the publisher and author do not offer any legal or
other professional advice.
In the case of a need for any such expertise consult with
the appropriate professional.
This book does not contain all information available on the

Contents

Contents

Contents

THE *Skinny*
HOT AIR FRYER
COOKBOOK
INTRODUCTION

Introduction

Hot Air Fryers are a fantastic new way of cooking that once discovered you won't be able to live without. This innovative and versatile appliance is a must for any modern kitchen and after you've tried it you won't look back! A Hot Air Fryer produces quick and easy healthy meals using a fraction of the oil required for traditional frying appliances. There is no preheating or mixing and it can cook a multitude of meals and snacks.....not just chips! Although having said that, chips are worthy of a special mention as hot air frying produces some of the best crispy chips you will ever taste using a tiny amount of oil and therefore reducing quantities of fat.

How Does Hot Air Frying Work?

Rather than the more traditional method of deep-frying, a hot air fryer uses very hot air (up to 200ºc) to circulate around the food so it cooks quickly with a crispy outer edge. As a hot air fryer requires no manual stirring or shaking it allows you to get on with other things while it cooks your perfect meal.

How Can It Produce Fried Food With So Little Oil?

The hot air circulation is so incredibly effective that there really is no need for vast quantities of oil to cook your food. One spoonful of oil is enough, making it the healthiest way to fry.

Will Fried Food Taste Different Using A Hot Air Fryer?

If anything it will taste better than the fried food you are accustomed to eating. Hot Air Fryers are designed to reduce the quantity of fat used in cooking without affecting the taste and whilst preserving flavour.

Cleaner, Safer, Healthier

Hot Air Fryers require only a spoonful of oil, which is around 100 times less than that used in a traditional deep fat fryer. Fresh oil is used each time you cook so there is no reusable oil creating strong odours and smoke – in fact hot air fryers are odourless. Using less oil is not only a healthier way to cook but also safer compared to traditional deep fat fryers. Most hot air fryers also pause the cooking process when the lid is lifted allowing you to add ingredients or seasoning safely.

Tips

Here are some useful hints and tips to get the best out of your hot air fryer:

• When making chips don't make them too long as they can get broken if your hot air fryer has a paddle.
• Rinse the chips well before adding to your hot air fryer to remove as much starch as possible.
• Thoroughly dry the chips before adding to the hot air fryer to prevent any scorching.
• Remove your chips promptly when the cooking process is complete to ensure they stay crispy.
• Clean your appliance after each use. All the parts should easily come apart and are usually dishwasher safe.
• Do not use any abrasive materials or cleaning products as this can damage the non-stick coating.
• Cut vegetables into small pieces to make sure they cook properly.
• Onions should be thinly sliced and separated.
• Read the manufacturers instructions. It sounds obvious but take some time to learn about all the functions of your hot air fryer before using it. Not only will this make it easier and more fun to use but it will also ensure you stay within

the warranty terms and conditions should any problems with the appliance occur.

Our Recipes
In keeping with the effortless nature of hot air frying, all our recipes are easy to follow with minimal preparation and cooking times.

We use a wide variety of fresh and inexpensive lower calorie/lower fat ingredients, all of which can be sourced from your local supermarket. We've limited the need for too many one-off store cupboard ingredients, which you are unlikely to use again and can be expensive.

While we recommend following the method for each of our recipes, we do encourage you to experiment with ingredients to suit your own taste, budget or according to what you have to hand in your kitchen. Don't be put off if you don't have one of the ingredients, try substituting with a different cut of meat, herb or spice. Cooking with your hot air fryer should be enjoyable and the more you try new things, the more fun you will have.

Please note:
• If your hot air fryer has a temperature control, set it to 180C/350F. If your appliance uses a preset temperature then disregard the temperature setting in each recipe method.
• Some hot air frying appliances require pre-heating. If this is the case, follow the manufacturers instructions prior to following our recipes.
• If your appliance does not automatically stir the ingredients then you should manually do this to ensure

even cooking. Use a wooden or plastic utensil to prevent any damage to the non-stick surface of your device.

We hope you enjoy the recipes in **The Skinny Hot Air Fryer Cookbook**. You may also enjoy more hot air frying recipes in **The Skinny ActiFry Cookbook**.

Skinny
HOT AIR FRYER
EASY LUNCHES

Fried Squid Rings With Lime

- Serves 4
- Cooking Time: 10-12 mins

Ingredients:

500g/1lb 2oz squid flesh cut into 1cm
½inch wide rings
1 tbsp plain/all purpose flour
½ tsp garlic powder
2 tsp olive oil or sunflower oil
Lime wedges to serve
Salt & pepper to taste

Method:

1. If your hot air fryer has a temperature control set it to 180C/350F.
2. Pat dry the squid rings and coat with the flour and garlic powder.
3. Place in the hot air fryer with the oil and cook for 10-12 minutes or until crispy and cooked through.
4. Season and serve with the lime wedges.

You could also try this recipe using lemon or lime infused olive oil.

Spanish Paprika Prawns

Ingredients:

500g/1lb 2oz peeled king prawns/
jumbo shrimp
1 tbsp paprika
3 garlic cloves, peeled & thinly sliced
2 onions, sliced
2 tsp olive oil or sunflower oil
Salt & pepper to taste

- Serves 4
- Cooking Time: 15-17 mins

Method:

1. If your hot air fryer has a temperature control set it to 180C/350F.
2. Pat dry the prawns and place in a plastic bag with the paprika.
3. Shake the bag really well until the prawns are completely covered.
4. Add the garlic, onions & oil to the hot air fryer and cook for 5 minutes.
5. Add the prawns and cook for a further 10-12 minutes or until the prawns are pink and cooked through.
6. Season and serve.

This is a popular tapas dish. Add a little lemon juice if you like.

Double Chilli Prawns & Green Beans

Ingredients:

500g/1lb 2oz peeled king prawns/ jumbo shrimp
1 tsp cayenne pepper
1 red chilli, deseeded and finely chopped
2 tsp olive oil or sunflower oil
200g/7oz green beans, roughly chopped
Salt & pepper to taste

Method:

1. If your hot air fryer has a temperature control set it to 180C/350F.
2. Pat dry the prawns and combine well with the cayenne pepper.
3. Place the prawns in the hot air fryer along with the oil, sliced chilli and green beans.
4. Cook for 13-15 minutes or until the prawns are pink and cooked through.

Lime wedges and flat bread make good accompaniments to this lunchtime dish.

Chicken 'Doner'

Ingredients:

• Serves 4
• Cooking Time: 20-25 mins

1 tbsp Worcestershire sauce/A1
steak sauce
1 tsp dried oregano
2 tbsp olive oil
3 garlic cloves, crushed
Zest & juice of ½ lemon
500g/1lb 2oz free range skinless
chicken breast, cut into 3 cm square
cubes
1 onion, sliced
1 red pepper, deseeded & sliced
4 large pitta breads
1 baby gem/romaine lettuce
shredded
2 large tomatoes, sliced
Salt & pepper to taste

Method:

1. If your hot air fryer has a temperature control set it to 180C/350F.
2. Combine together the Worcestershire sauce, oregano, olive oil & garlic along with the juice and zest of ½ lemon in a large bowl.
3. Add the cubed chicken, cover and leave to marinate for an hour or two.
4. Remove the marinated meat from the bowl, place in the hot air fryer along with the onions and sliced peppers and cook for 20-25 or until the chicken is cooked through.
5. Pile the meat and peppers into the pitta breads along with the lettuce & sliced tomatoes.

Some hot Tabasco sauce makes a good addition to this dish. Add as much as you dare!

Spring Green Gnocchi

Ingredients:

2 garlic cloves, crushed
1 onion, sliced
2 tsp olive oil or sunflower oil
200g/7oz spring greens, shredded
800g/1¾lb premade gnocchi
½ tsp salt
2 tbsp freshly grated Parmesan cheese
2 tsp low fat 'butter' spread
Salt & pepper to taste

Method:

1. If your hot air fryer has a temperature control set it to 180C/350F.
2. Place the garlic, onions & oil in the hot air fryer and cook for 5 minutes.
3. Add the spring greens, gnocchi & salt and cook for 20-25 minutes or until the gnocchi is crispy on the outside and tender on the inside.
4. Stir through the grated Parmesan and 'butter' and serve immediately.

The spring greens should be shredded as thinly as possible, a quick whizz in the food processor before cooking will do the trick.

Turkey Tacos

Ingredients:

• Serves 4
• Cooking Time: 35-40 mins

1 onion, finely chopped
2 garlic cloves, crushed
1 red pepper, deseeded & sliced
2 tsp olive oil or sunflower oil
400g/14oz leanturkey mince/ground turkey
200g/7oz tinned chopped tomatoes
1 tbsp tomato puree/paste
½ tsp each paprika, cumin, cayenne pepper & coriander/cilantro
1 iceberg lettuce, shredded
8 taco shells
Salt & pepper to taste

Method:

1. If your hot air fryer has a temperature control set it to 180C/350F.
2. Place the onions, garlic, pepper & oil in the hot air fryer and cook for 5 minutes.
3. Add the turkey mince, chopped tomatoes, tomato puree & dried spices and cook for 30-35 minutes or until everything is cooked through and piping hot.
4. Season and serve in taco shells with the shredded lettuce.

Creamy fat free Greek yoghurt and grated cheese and good with this taco recipe.

Ground Lamb & Peas

Ingredients:

1 onion, finely chopped
2 garlic cloves, crushed
2 tsp olive oil or sunflower oil
400g/14oz lean lamb mince/ground lamb
200g/7oz vine ripened tomatoes, roughly chopped
2 tbsp tomato ketchup
1 tsp each ground coriander/cilantro, cumin & chilli powder
200g/7oz peas
2 tbsp water
2 tbsp freshly chopped coriander/cilantro
Salt & pepper to taste

Method:

1. If your hot air fryer has a temperature control set it to 180C/350F.
2. Place the onions, garlic & oil in the hot air fryer and cook for 5 minutes.
3. Add the mince, chopped tomatoes, ketchup, dried spices, peas & water and cook for 25-35 minutes or until everything is cooked through and piping hot (add a little more water during cooking if needed).
4. Season and serve with chopped coriander sprinkled over the top.

This can also be served with rice and/or chapatti bread to make a hearty supper.

Five Spice Steak & Savoy Cabbage

Ingredients:

1 onion, sliced
2 garlic cloves, crushed
1 tsp Chinese Five Spice powder
2 carrots, cut into thin matchsticks
2 tsp olive oil or sunflower oil
400g/14oz lean sirloin steak, sliced
into strips
1 savoy/Napa cabbage, shredded
1 tbsp soy sauce
Salt & pepper to taste

- Serves 4
- Cooking Time: 15-17 mins

Method:

1. If your hot air fryer has a temperature control set it to 180C/350F.
2. Place the onions, garlic, 5 spice powder, carrots & oil in the hot air fryer and cook for 5 minutes.
3. Add the steak, shredded cabbage & soy sauce and cook for 10-12 minutes or until the steak is cooked through and the cabbage is tender.
4. Season and serve.

Reduce the steak cooking time if you prefer your beef rare.

21

Crispy Chicken Fried Rice

- Serves 4
- Cooking Time: 19-21

Ingredients:

200g/7oz cooked chicken, finely chopped
125g/4oz cooked ham, finely chopped
1 onion, chopped
2 garlic cloves, crushed
1 red pepper, deseeded & finely chopped
125g/4oz peas
2 tsp olive oil or sunflower oil
1 tbsp water
500g/1lb 2oz precooked rice
2 free range eggs, lightly beaten
1 tbsp soy sauce
2 tbsp freshly chopped coriander/cilantro
Salt & pepper to taste

Method:

1. If your hot air fryer has a temperature control set it to 180C/350F.
2. Place the chicken, ham, onions, garlic, pepper, peas, oil & water in the hot air fryer and cook for 12 minutes.
3. Add the rice, eggs & soy sauce and cook for 7-9 minutes or until everything is cooked through and piping hot.
4. Season and serve with the chopped coriander sprinkled on top.

Feel free to substitute the chicken or ham with pork or turkey.

Pork Tenderloin & Spring Vegetables

Ingredients:

- Serves 4
- Cooking Time: 23-24 mins

500g/1lb 2oz free range pork
tenderloin, sliced
2 garlic cloves, finely sliced
2 red peppers, deseeded & sliced
1 onion, sliced
1 tbsp water
2 tsp olive oil or sunflower oil
125g/4oz baby corn
125g/4oz green beans
125g/4oz carrots, sliced into batons
300g/11oz beansprouts
Salt & pepper to taste

Method:

1. If your hot air fryer has a temperature control set it to 180C/350F.
2. Season the pork. Place the garlic, sliced peppers, onions, water & oil in the hot air fryer and cook for 5 minutes.
3. Add the mini corn, French beans & carrots and cook for 15 minutes.
4. Add the beansprouts and cook for a further 3-4 minutes or until the pork is cooked through and the beansprouts and vegetables are piping hot.
5. Season and serve.

Pork tenderloin is a great low-fat meat. Use free-range pork if you can to get the best flavour.

Creamy Steak & Spinach

Ingredients:

2 onions, sliced

2 tsp olive oil or sunflower oil

1 tsp paprika

400g/14oz lean sirloin steak, sliced

200g/7oz tinned condensed mushroom soup

200g/7oz spinach leaves

Salt & pepper to taste

Method:

1. If your hot air fryer has a temperature control set it to 180C/350F.
2. Place the onions & oil in the hot air fryer and cook for 5 minutes.
3. Add the paprika & steak and cook for 10 minutes.
4. Add the soup & spinach and cook for a further 5-10 minutes or until the steak is cooked through and the dish is piping hot.
5. Season and serve.

Condensed soup is a handy store cupboard ingredient for easy weekday lunches and suppers.

Parmesan & Hazelnut Chicken Thighs

Ingredients:

- Serves 4
- Cooking Time: 30-40 mins

2 garlic cloves, crushed
½ tsp each salt & brown sugar
75g/3oz Parmesan cheese, grated
2 tbsp hazelnuts, very finely chopped
12 free range bone-in chicken thighs
2 tsp olive oil or sunflower oil
Salt & pepper to taste

Method:

1. If your hot air fryer has a temperature control set it to 180C/350F.
2. Combine the garlic cloves, salt, sugar, grated cheese & chopped hazelnuts together and rub into the chicken thighs.
3. Place the chicken & oil in the hot air fryer and cook for 30-40 minutes or until the chicken is cooked through, crispy and piping hot.
4. Season and serve.

This is lovely served with a creamy aioli sauce and mashed potatoes.

Chicken Pittas

- Serves 4
- Cooking Time: 15-18 mins

Ingredients:

500g/1lb 2oz free range skinless
chicken breast, sliced
2 tsp olive oil or sunflower oil
3 garlic cloves, finely sliced
60ml/¼ cup chicken stock
1 tsp each turmeric & paprika
½ tsp salt
150g/5oz precooked rice
2 tbsp freshly chopped flat leaf
parsley
4 pitta bread
Salt & pepper to taste

Method:

1. If your hot air fryer has a temperature control set it to 180C/350F.
2. Add all the ingredients to the hot air fryer, except the rice, parsley & pitta bread.
3. Cook for 12-14 minutes or until the chicken is cooked through.
4. Add the rice and cook for a further 3-4 minutes.
5. Season well and load into the pittas.
6. Sprinkle with parsley and serve.

This is a lovely filling dish, which can be served for lunch or bulked up with a salad for dinner.

26

Indian Spiced Wings

Ingredients:

2 red chillies, deseeded
1 red pepper, deseeded
2 tsp medium curry powder
2 garlic cloves
½ tsp each salt & brown sugar
16 free range chicken wings
1 tsp olive oil or sunflower oil
Salt & pepper to taste

Method:

1. If your hot air fryer has a temperature control set it to 180C/350F.
2. Place the chillies, peppers, curry powder, garlic, salt & sugar in a food processor and pulse until blended.
3. Pierce the wings, smother with the curry blend and leave to marinate for an hour or two (don't worry if you don't have time for this, it will still taste good).
4. Place the chicken wings & oil in the hot air fryer and cook for 25-35 minutes or until the chicken wings are cooked through and piping hot.
5. Season and serve.

This dish is even better served with a side dip of low fat Greek yoghurt and chopped coriander.

Tequila & Cayenne Chicken

Ingredients:

2 red onions, sliced
2 tsp olive oil or sunflower oil
500g/1lb 2oz free range skinless chicken breast, sliced
2 tbsp tomato paste/puree
3 tbsp tequila
2 tsp cayenne pepper
½ tsp each salt & brown sugar
4 taco shells
1 iceberg lettuce, shredded
2 tbsp fat free Greek yoghurt
Salt & pepper to taste

Method:

1. If your hot air fryer has a temperature control set it to 180C/350F.
2. Place the onions & oil in the hot air fryer and cook for 5 minutes.
3. Add the chicken, tomato puree, tequila, cayenne pepper, salt & sugar and cook for a further 15-17 minutes or until the chicken is cooked through and piping hot.
4. Season and serve in tacos with the shredded lettuce and Greek yogurt.

Use a little white wine vinegar as an alternative to tequila if you wish.

Cajun & Coriander Drumsticks

Ingredients:

• Serves 4
• Cooking Time: 30-35 mins

1 tsp each ground ginger, allspice & paprika
2 garlic cloves, crushed
12 free range chicken drumsticks
1 tsp olive oil or sunflower oil
2 tbsp freshly chopped coriander/cilantro
Lemon wedges to serve
Salt & pepper to taste

Method:

1. If your hot air fryer has a temperature control set it to 180C/350F.
2. Mix together the dry spices and garlic to make a Cajun rub.
3. Pierce the chicken drumsticks and rub the Cajun spices into the skin. Leave to marinate for an hour or two.
4. After this time place the drumsticks & oil in the hot air fryer and cook for 30-35 minutes or until the chicken is cooked through and piping hot.
5. Serve with the chopped coriander sprinkled over the top and lemon wedges on the side.

Feel free to use a pre-made Cajun rub if that's what you have to hand.

Fennel Fried Wings

- Serves 4
- Cooking Time: 30-35 mins

Ingredients:

3 garlic cloves, crushed
1 tsp fennel seeds, crushed
½ tsp salt
1 tbsp tomato ketchup
16 free range chicken wings
1 tsp olive oil
Lemon wedges to serve
Salt & pepper to taste

Method:

1. If your hot air fryer has a temperature control set it to 180C/350F.
2. Mix together the garlic cloves, fennel seeds, salt & ketchup and smother all over the chicken wings.
3. Place the chicken & oil in the hot air fryer and cook for 30-35 minutes or until the chicken is cooked through and piping hot.
4. Season and serve with lemon wedges.

The fennel seeds, garlic and ketchup combine to make a simple & potent BBQ style covering. Serve with a fresh tomato & onion salad.

Beef & Rosemary Meatballs

Ingredients:

• Serves 4
• Cooking Time: 20-25 mins

500g/1lb 2oz lean beef mince/
ground beef
2 garlic cloves, crushed
2 tbsp fresh breadcrumbs
1 tsp dried rosemary
½ tsp each brown sugar & salt
2 tsp olive oil or sunflower oil
2 red peppers, deseeded & sliced
1 onion, sliced
300g/11oz ripe cherry tomatoes,
halved
1 tbsp water
2 tbsp tomato puree/paste
Salt & pepper to taste

Method:

1. If your hot air fryer has a temperature control set it to 180C/350F.
2. Put the beef mince, garlic cloves, breadcrumbs, rosemary, sugar & salt in a food processor and pulse a few times until combined.
3. Take the mixture out and form into small meatballs with your hands.
4. Place the meatballs, peppers & onions in the hot air fryer and cook for 10 minutes.
5. Add the cherry tomatoes, water & puree and cook for a further 10-15 or until the meatballs are cooked through and piping hot.
6. Season and serve.

This dish is great served with spaghetti or noodles or a side dish of steamed spinach.

Chorizo & Scallop Watercress Wraps

Ingredients:

2 onions, sliced

4 garlic cloves, peeled & finely sliced

1 tsp paprika

1 red chilli, finely chopped

200g/7oz chorizo sausage, diced

1 tsp olive oil or sunflower oil

500g/1lb 2oz shelled, prepared scallops

4 soft tortilla wraps

125g/40z watercress

Lemon wedges to serve

Salt & pepper to taste

Method:

1. If your hot air fryer has a temperature control set it to 180C/350F.

2. Place the onions, garlic, paprika, chilli, chorizo & oil in the hot air fryer and cook for 8 minutes.

3. Add the scallops and cook for a further 3-5 minutes or until the scallops are cooked through and piping hot.

4. Season and serve with the tortilla wraps, watercress and lemon wedges.

Watercress is a great salad 'filler' for this wrap. Radicchio would work well too.

Ginger Scallops & Zucchini

Ingredients:

200g/7oz baby courgettes/zucchini
thinly sliced
2 tsp freshly grated ginger
2 tsp olive oil or sunflower oil
500g/1lb 2oz shelled, prepared
scallops
Lemon wedges to serve
Salt & pepper to taste

- Serves 4
- Cooking Time: 17-19 mins

Method:

1. If your hot air fryer has a temperature control set it to 180C/350F.
2. Season the courgettes slices and place in the hot air fryer along with the oil and ginger.
3. Cook for 15 minutes.
4. Add the scallops and cook for a further 2-4 minutes or until the scallops are cooked through.
5. Season and serve with lemon wedges.

Add some freshly chopped flat leaf parsley and some dried chilli flakes if you like.

Salt & Pepper Chicken

- Serves 4
- Cooking Time: 10-14 mins

Ingredients:

400g/14oz free range skinless
chicken breast, sliced
1 tsp dried chilli flakes
1 tbsp ground black pepper
1 tbsp honey
1 tsp salt
2 tsp olive oil or sunflower oil
Lime wedges to serve
Salt & pepper to taste

Method:

1. If your hot air fryer has a temperature control set it to 180C/350F.
2. Place the chicken, chilli flakes, pepper, honey and salt in a large bowl and combine really well.
3. Add to the hot air fryer along with the oil and cook for 10-14 minutes or until the chicken is cooked through.
4. Season and serve with lime wedges

Adjust the balance of chilli, salt and sweet honey to suit your own taste.

Aubergine & Chilli Stir-Fried Omelette

Ingredients:

- Serves 4
- Cooking Time: 28-30 mins

1 aubergine/egg plant, cut into cubes
1 red chilli, deseeded and finely chopped
1 onion, sliced
2 tsp olive oil
10 free range eggs, lightly beaten
2 tbsp freshly chopped chives
Salt & pepper to taste

Method:

1. If your hot air fryer has a temperature control set it to 180C/350F.
2. Place the aubergine, chilli, onions & oil in the hot air fryer and cook for 20 minutes.
3. Add the eggs & chives and cook for a further 8-10 minutes or until everything is tender and piping hot.
4. Season and serve.

Courgettes and/or peppers are also good alternatives for this scrambled omelette in place of the aubergine.

Skinny

HOT AIR FRYER

SIMPLE SUPPERS

Prawn, Lime & Peanut Stir-Fry

- Serves 4
- Cooking Time: 22-23 mins

Ingredients:

1 onion, sliced

2 garlic cloves, peeled & finely sliced

2 tsp freshly grated ginger

1 Chinese cabbage, shredded

2 red peppers, deseeded & sliced

2 tsp olive oil or sunflower oil

400g/14oz peeled king prawns/ jumbo shrimp

1 tbsp each honey & lime juice

2 tbsp soy sauce

150g/5oz spinach leaves

300g/11oz precooked noodles

125g/4oz unsalted peanuts, chopped

Salt & pepper to taste

Method:

1. If your hot air fryer has a temperature control set it to 180C/350F.
2. Place the onions, garlic, ginger, pak choi, peppers & oil in the hot air fryer and cook for 10 minutes.
3. Add the prawns, honey & soy and cook for a further 8 minutes.
4. Add the lime juice, spinach & noodles and cook for a further 4-5 minutes or until the prawns are cooked through and the spinach & noodles are piping hot.
5. Season and serve with the chopped peanuts on top.

Chicken also works well for this simple stir-fry along with a little chopped coriander.

Hong Kong Style Chicken & Rice

Ingredients:

- Serves 4
- Cooking Time: 22-24 mins

250ml/1 cup pineapple juice
2-3 tsp cornflour/cornstarch
100g/3½oz tinned pineapple chunks,
drained
1 onion, sliced
2 tsp freshly grated ginger
1 red pepper, deseeded & sliced
2 tsp olive oil or sunflower oil
500g/1lb 2oz free range skinless
chicken breast, cut into strips
150g/5oz fresh beansprouts
400g/14oz hot precooked rice for
serving
Salt & pepper to taste

Method:

1. If your hot air fryer has a temperature control set it to 180C/350F.
2. First mix together the pineapple juice and cornflower to make a smooth paste (adjust the quantity of corn flour to get the consistency right).
3. Place the pineapples chunks, onions, ginger, peppers & oil in the hot air fryer and cook for 10 minutes.
4. Add the chicken and pineapple paste and cook for a further 10 minutes.
5. Add the beansprouts and cook for 2-4 minutes or until the chicken is cooked through and the beansprouts are piping hot. Season and serve piled on top of the cooked rice.

Add a pinch of sea salt and brown sugar if you need to balance the flavour of dish.

Chicken, Raisins & Rice

Ingredients:

2 onions, sliced

4 garlic cloves, crushed

2 tsp olive oil or sunflower oil

400g/14oz free range skinless chicken breast, sliced

150g/5oz raisins

4 large tomatoes, roughly chopped

300g/11oz precooked rice

4 tbsp freshly chopped coriander/cilantro

Salt & pepper to taste

Method:

1. If your hot air fryer has a temperature control set it to 180C/350F.
2. Place the onions & garlic in the hot air fryer and cook for 8 minutes.
3. Add the sliced chicken, raisins & tomatoes and cook for 10 minutes.
4. Add the pre-cooked rice and cook for a further 2-4 minutes or until everything is cooked through and piping hot. Season and serve with chopped coriander.

Add a little stock to the fryer if you feel it needs it during cooking.

Chicken & Pineapple

Ingredients:

• Serves 4
• Cooking Time: 17-19 mins

2 onions, sliced

2 garlic cloves, crushed

2 carrots, cut into matchsticks

2 tsp olive oil or sunflower oil

500g/1lb 2oz free range skinless
chicken breast, cut into strips

125g/4oz fresh or tinned pineapple,
finely chopped

3 tbsp chicken stock

300g/11oz hot precooked rice for
serving

1 bunch spring onions/scallions,
sliced lengthways into ribbons

Salt & pepper to taste

Method:

1. If your hot air fryer has a temperature control set it to 180C/350F.
2. Place the onions, garlic, carrots & oil in the hot air fryer and cook for 5 minutes.
3. Add the chicken, pineapple & stock and cook for 12-14 minutes or until the chicken is cooked through.
4. Season and serve with the rice and spring onion ribbons.

Add a little chopped flat leaf parsley if you wish.

Red Thai Beef

Ingredients:

2 onions, sliced

2 garlic cloves, crushed

1 red pepper, deseeded & sliced

125g/4oz mushrooms, sliced

2 carrots, cut into matchsticks

2 tsp olive oil or sunflower oil

500g/1lb 2oz lean sirloin steak, cut into strips

2 tbsp Thai red curry paste

2 tbsp coconut cream

2 tbsp freshly chopped coriander/ cilantro

Salt & pepper to taste

Method:

1. If your hot air fryer has a temperature control set it to 180C/350F.
2. Place the onions, garlic, peppers, mushrooms, carrots & oil in the hot air fryer and cook for 5 minutes.
3. Add the beef & curry paste and cook for 10 minutes.
4. Add the coconut cream and cook for a minute or two longer or until everything is cooked through and piping hot.
5. Season and serve with the chopped coriander sprinkled over the top.

Serve with boiled rice or noodles along with some lime wedges if you like.

Chicken & Mange Tout Teriyaki Noodles

Ingredients:

1 onion, sliced
2 carrots, cut into matchsticks
2 red or yellow peppers, sliced
2 garlic cloves, crushed
2 tsp olive oil or sunflower oil
400g/14oz free range skinless chicken breast, cubed
200g/7oz mange tout
2 tbsp teriyaki sauce
1 tbsp soy sauce
300g/11oz precooked or straight-to-wok noodles
1 bunch spring onions/scallions, sliced lengthways into ribbons
Salt & pepper to taste

Method:

1. If your hot air fryer has a temperature control set it to 180C/350F.
2. Place the onions, carrots, peppers, garlic & oil in the hot air fryer and cook for 10 minutes.
3. Add the sliced chicken, mange tout & teriyaki sauce and cook for 5 minutes.
4. Add the soy sauce and noodles and cook for 6-8 minutes or until everything is cooked through and piping hot.
5. Season and serve with the spring onion ribbons sprinkled on top.

Increase the teriyaki sauce quantity if you want a particularly sticky & sweet dish.

Tenderstem Broccoli & Chicken Rice

Ingredients:

2 onions, sliced

1 red chilli, finely chopped

3 garlic cloves, crushed

250g/9oz tenderstem broccoli/
broccolini, roughly chopped

2 tsp olive oil or sunflower oil

400g/14oz free range skinless
chicken breast, sliced

1 free range egg

300g/11oz precooked rice

Salt & pepper to taste

Method:

1. If your hot air fryer has a temperature control set it to 180C/350F.
2. Place the onions, chillies, garlic, chopped broccoli & oil in the hot air fryer and cook for 10 minutes.
3. Add the sliced chicken and cook for a further 10 minutes.
4. Add the cooked rice and egg and cook 3-5 minutes or until everything is cooked through and piping hot.
5. Season and serve.

Add some freshly chopped mint or basil as a garnish if you wish.

Spiced Beef & Apricots

Ingredients:

1 onion, sliced
2 tsp freshly grated ginger
2 garlic cloves, crushed
2 tsp olive oil or sunflower oil
400g/14oz lean sirloin steak, cut into strips
50g/2oz dried apricots, finely chopped
60ml/¼ cup beef stock
½ tsp each chilli powder & ground coriander/cilantro
2 tbsp freshly chopped coriander/cilantro
400g/14oz precooked rice
Salt & pepper to taste

Method:

1. If your hot air fryer has a temperature control set it to 180C/350F.
2. Place the onions, ginger, garlic & oil in the hot air fryer and cook for 5 minutes.
3. Add the steak, apricots and stock along with the dry spices and cook for 10 minutes.
4. Add the cooked rice and chopped coriander and cook for a further 5-7 minutes or until everything is cooked through and piping hot.
5. Season and serve.

Fresh ginger and garlic are a great combination and make a solid flavour base for so many spiced dishes.

Pepperoni Rice

Ingredients:

1 onion, sliced

2 garlic cloves, crushed

2 green peppers, finely chopped

200g/7oz pepperoni, finely chopped

2 tsp olive oil or sunflower oil

1 tsp paprika

400g/14oz precooked rice

2 free range eggs, lightly beaten

150g/5oz tinned pineapple, finely chopped

Salt & pepper to taste

Method:

1. If your hot air fryer has a temperature control set it to 180C/350F.
2. Place the onions, garlic, peppers, pepperoni & oil in the hot air fryer and cook for 10 minutes.
3. Add the paprika, rice, eggs & pineapple and cook for 8-12 minutes or until everything is cooked through and piping hot.
4. Season and serve.

Use any type of salami you wish for this recipe in place of pepperoni.

Chicken & Chickpeas

Ingredients:

• Serves 4
• Cooking Time: 15-20 mins

1 onion, sliced
2 garlic cloves, crushed
2 tsp olive oil or sunflower oil
500g/1lb 2oz free range skinless chicken breast, cubed
200g/7oz ripe cherry tomatoes, halved
400g/14oz tinned chickpeas, drained
1 tbsp tomato puree/paste
1 tsp turmeric
60ml/¼ cup chicken stock
2 tbsp freshly chopped flat leaf parsley
Salt & pepper to taste

Method:

1. If your hot air fryer has a temperature control set it to 180C/350F.
2. Place the onions, garlic & oil in the hot air fryer and cook for 5 minutes.
3. Add the sliced chicken, cherry tomatoes, chickpeas, tomato puree, turmeric & stock and cook for 10-15 minutes or until everything is cooked through and piping hot.
4. Season and serve with the chopped parsley sprinkled on top.

Add a little chopped fresh red chilli to garnish if you like.

47

Lamb & Mint Meatballs With Sweet Potatoes

Ingredients:

500g/1lb 2oz lean lamb mince/ ground lamb
2 garlic cloves, crushed
2 tbsp freshly chopped mint
2 tbsp fresh breadcrumbs
1 tsp paprika
½ tsp each brown sugar & salt
400g/14oz sweet potatoes, peeled, cubed & patted dry
2 tsp olive oil or sunflower oil
200g/7oz peas
Salt & pepper to taste

Method:

1. If your hot air fryer has a temperature control set it to 180C/350F.
2. Put the lamb mince, garlic cloves, mint, breadcrumbs, paprika, sugar & salt in a food processor and pulse a few times until combined.
3. Take the mixture out and form into small meatballs with your hands.
4. Place the cubed sweet potatoes in the hot air fryer and cook for 15 minutes.
5. Add the lamb meatballs & and cook for a further 20 minutes or until the meatballs are cooked through and the potatoes are tender.
6. Add the peas and cook for 5 minutes or until tender.
7. Season and serve.

If you are using frozen peas add these to the hot air fryer when you add the meatballs.

48

Oyster Sauce Chicken & Noodles

Ingredients:

• Serves 4
• Cooking Time: 21-23 mins

1 onion, sliced
2 tsp olive oil or sunflower oil
500g/1lb 2oz free range skinless chicken breast, sliced
1 tbsp water
200g/7oz tinned sweetcorn, drained
1 head savoy/Napa cabbage, shredded
2 tbsp oyster sauce
300g/11oz precooked or straight-to-wok noodles
1 bunch spring onions/scallions, sliced lengthways into ribbons
Salt & pepper to taste

Method:

1. If your hot air fryer has a temperature control set it to 180C/350F.
2. Place the onions & oil in the hot air fryer and cook for 5 minutes.
3. Add the chicken, water, sweetcorn, shredded cabbage & oyster sauce and cook for 14 minutes.
4. Add the noodles and cook for a further 2-4 minutes or until the chicken is cooked through and the noodles are piping hot.
5. Season and serve with the spring onion ribbons.

Oyster sauce adds a lovely depth to a stir-fry 'and is widely available in most shops & supermarkets.

Sweet Five Spice Chicken

- Serves 4
- Cooking Time: 19-23 mins

Ingredients:

500g/1lb 2oz free range skinless chicken breast, sliced
1 tsp Chinese Five Spice powder
1 onion, sliced
2 red peppers, deseeded & sliced
2 tsp olive oil or sunflower oil
1 tbsp soy sauce
1 tsp honey
1 pointed green/Napa cabbage, shredded
300g/11oz precooked or straight-to-wok noodles
Salt & pepper to taste

Method:

1. If your hot air fryer has a temperature control set it to 180C/350F.
2. First rub the 5 spice powder onto the chicken pieces.
3. Place the onions, peppers & oil in the hot air fryer and cook for 5 minutes.
4. Add the chicken, soy sauce, honey & cabbage and cook for 12-14 minutes or until the chicken is cooked through.
5. Add the noodles and cook for a further 2-4 minutes or until everything is combined and piping hot.
6. Season and serve.

Green pointed cabbage works particularly well for this dish but you could substitute with kale or spinach if you wish.

Spinach & Chicken Rice

Ingredients:

• Serves 4
• Cooking Time: 19-21 mins

2 onions, sliced

2 garlic cloves, crushed

2 tsp olive oil or sunflower oil

400g/14oz free range skinless chicken breast, sliced

200g/7oz vine ripened chopped tomatoes

2 tbsp sundried tomato puree/paste

200g/7oz spinach leaves

½ tsp salt

300g/11oz precooked rice

Lemon wedges to serve

Salt & pepper to taste

Method:

1. If your hot air fryer has a temperature control set it to 180C/350F.
2. Place the onions, garlic & oil in the hot air fryer and cook for 5 minutes.
3. Add the chicken, tomatoes, puree, spinach & salt and cook for 12 minutes.
4. Add the rice and cook for a further 2-4 minutes or until the chicken is cooked through and the rice is piping hot.
5. Season and serve.

If you are short of time handy packs of pre-cooked rice are available in most supermarkets.

Lime & Coconut Chicken Noodles

- Serves 4
- Cooking Time: 20-22 mins

Ingredients:

2 garlic cloves, finely sliced
1 onion, sliced
2 tsp coconut oil
200g/7oz asparagus tips, chopped
1 tbsp tomato puree/paste
½ tsp each ground cumin & salt
1 tbsp lime juice
1 tbsp coconut cream
500g/1lb 2oz free range skinless chicken breast, cubed
300g/11oz precooked or straight-to-wok noodles
2 tbsp freshly chopped flat leaf parsley
Salt & pepper to taste

Method:

1. If your hot air fryer has a temperature control set it to 180C/350F.
2. Place the garlic, onions & oil in the hot air fryer and cook for 5 minutes.
3. Add the asparagus, puree, cumin & salt and cook for 3 minutes.
4. Add the chicken, lime juice & coconut cream and cook for a further 10-12 minutes.
5. Add the noodles and cook for 2 minutes or until the chicken is cooked through and the noodles are piping hot.
6. Season, sprinkle with chopped parsley and serve.

Any sliced greens can be used in place of the asparagus.

Lemon Chicken & Rice

Ingredients:

• Serves 4
• Cooking Time: 18-20 mins

500g/1lb 2oz free range skinless
chicken breast, cubed
1 tsp cornflour/cornstarch
3 garlic cloves, finely sliced
1 onion, sliced
2 orange peppers, deseeded & sliced
2 tsp olive oil or sunflower oil
Zest & Juice ½ lemon
60ml/¼ chicken stock
2 tbsp freshly chopped coriander/
cilantro
300g/11oz hot precooked rice for
serving
Salt & pepper to taste

Method:

1. If your hot air fryer has a temperature control set it to 180C/350F.
2. Season the chicken & dust evenly with the corn flour.
3. Place the garlic, onions, peppers & oil in the hot air fryer and cook for 5 minutes.
4. Add the dusted chicken and cook for 8 minutes.
5. Add the lemon juice, zest & stock to the hot air fryer and cook for a further 5-7 minutes or until the chicken is cooked through and piping hot.
6. Season and serve with the hot pre-cooked rice.

Add a little more or less lemon to suit your own taste.

Beef Korma

Ingredients:

2 garlic cloves, finely sliced
1 onion, sliced
200g/7oz peas
2 tsp olive oil or sunflower oil
1 tbsp mild curry powder
½ tsp salt
1 tbsp tomato puree/paste
180ml/¾ cup tomato passata/sauce
500g/1lb 2oz lean sirloin steak, sliced
3 tbsp fat free Greek yoghurt
2 tbsp freshly chopped almond flakes
Salt & pepper to taste

Method:

1. If your hot air fryer has a temperature control set it to 180C/350F.
2. Place the garlic, onions, peas & oil in the hot air fryer and cook for 5 minutes.
3. Add the curry powder, salt, tomato puree, passata & steak and cook for 14-16 minutes or until the beef is cooked through and piping hot.
4. Season, stir through the yoghurt and serve with the chopped almond flakes.

Naan bread and sliced red onions make good accompaniments to this dish.

Scallop Stir-Fry

Ingredients:

- Serves 4
- Cooking Time: 17-18 mins

1 onion, sliced
1 garlic clove, crushed
2 tsp olive oil or sunflower oil
1 carrot, cut into matchsticks
1 chinese cabbage, shredded
125g/4oz peas
1 red pepper, deseeded & sliced
1 tbsp oyster sauce
2 tbsp Thai Fish sauce
1 tbsp soy sauce
500g/1lb 2oz prepared scallops
300g/11oz straight-to-wok noodles
A large bunch of spring onions/
scallions sliced lengthways
Salt & pepper to taste

Method:

1. If your hot air fryer has a temperature control set it to 180C/350F.
2. Place the onions, garlic & oil in the hot air fryer and cook for 6 minutes.
3. Add the carrot, cabbage, peppers & peas and cook for a further 5 minutes.
4. Add the oyster sauce, fish sauce, soy & scallops and cook for 3 minutes.
5. Add the noodles, cook for a further 3-4 minutes or until the scallops are cooked through.
6. Season & serve with the spring onions sprinkled over the top.

Precooked or Straight-to-wok noodles are widely available in most supermarkets.

Mini Turkey Meatballs

Ingredients:

500g/1lb 2oz lean turkey mince/ground turkey
1 tsp dried sage
1 garlic clove, crushed
2 tbsp fresh breadcrumbs
150g/5oz cheddar cheese, grated
2 tsp olive oil or sunflower oil
400g/14oz tomato passata/sauce
1 tbsp Worcestershire sauce/A1 steak sauce
½ tsp each brown sugar & salt
2 tbsp tomato puree/paste
Salt & pepper to taste

Method:

1. If your hot air fryer has a temperature control set it to 180C/350F.
2. Put the turkey mince, sage, garlic, breadcrumbs & cheese in a food processor and pulse a few times until combined.
3. Take the mixture out and form into mini meatballs (about 2-3cm wide) with your hands.
4. Place the meatballs in the hot air fryer and cook for 15 minutes.
5. Add the tomato passata, Worcestershire sauce, salt, sugar & puree and cooked a further 5-10 minutes or until the meatballs are cooked through and the sauce is piping hot.
6. Season and serve.

Use low fat cheddar cheese & serve with rice or spaghetti and lots of chopped flat leaf parsley.

Garlic & Ginger Beef Spinach

Ingredients:

• Serves 4
• Cooking Time: 11-13 mins

2 onions, sliced
8 garlic cloves, finely sliced
1 tbsp freshly grated ginger
2 tsp olive oil or vegetable oil
400g/14oz lean sirloin or rump steak, sliced
150g/5oz spinach leaves
300g/11oz precooked or 'straight-to-wok' noodles
1 tbsp tomato puree/paste
1 tbsp water
Salt & pepper to taste

Method:

1. If your hot air fryer has a temperature control set it to 180C/350F.
2. Place the onions, garlic, ginger & oil in the hot air fryer and cook for 5 minutes.
3. Add the steak and cook for 4 minutes.
4. Add the spinach, noodles, tomato puree & water and cook for a further 2-4 minutes or until everything is cooked through and piping hot.
5. Season and serve.

Chicken or pork also works well for this recipe. Add some fresh chilli if you like.

Ginger & Garlic Chicken

- Serves 4
- Cooking Time: 19-21 mins

Ingredients:

6 garlic cloves, finely sliced

1 tbsp freshly grated ginger

1 onion, sliced

2 tsp olive oil or sunflower oil

½ tsp each of salt & turmeric

200g/7oz asparagus tips, roughly chopped

500g/1lb 2oz free range skinless chicken breast, cubed

300g/11oz precooked rice

1 bunch spring onions/scallions, finely sliced

Salt & pepper to taste

Method:

1. If your hot air fryer has a temperature control set it to 180C/350F.
2. Place the garlic, ginger, onions & oil in the hot air fryer and cook for 5 minutes.
3. Add the salt, turmeric, asparagus & chicken and cook for 12-14 minutes or until the chicken is cooked through and piping hot.
4. Add the rice and cook for a further 2 minutes.
5. Season and serve with chopped spring onions on top.

Fresh ginger and garlic make a perfect combination for simple stir-fry dishes.

Skinny
HOT AIR FRYER
SIDES & SNACKS

Balsamic Asparagus

Ingredients:

400g/14oz asparagus tips
2 tsp olive oil or sunflower oil
1 tbsp balsamic vinegar
Salt & pepper to taste

Method:

1. If your hot air fryer has a temperature control set it to 180C/350F.
2. Place the asparagus, oil & balsamic vinegar in the hot air fryer.
3. Cook for 10-15 minutes or until tender.
4. Season and serve.

Asparagus is a delicious seasonal spring vegetable, which works really well in the hot air fryer.

Coconut Green Beans

Ingredients:

400g/14oz green beans
2 tsp coconut oil
Salt & pepper to taste

- Serves 4
- Cooking Time: 10-12 mins

Method:

1. If your hot air fryer has a temperature control set it to 180C/350F.
2. Place the green beans in the hot air fryer along with the coconut oil.
3. Cook for 10-12 minutes or until tender and cooked through.

Japanese edamame beans work really well for this recipe too, along with a little chopped chilli.

Crispy 'Ladies Fingers'

Ingredients:

400g/14oz okra
1 tbsp curry powder
2 tsp olive oil or sunflower oil
Salt & pepper to taste

Method:

1. If your hot air fryer has a temperature control set it to 180C/350F.
2. Slice the okra into really thin 'fingers', rinse in water and pat dry.
3. Combine with the curry powder and place in the hot air fryer along with the oil.
4. Cook for 15-25 minutes, or until the okra is tender and cooked through.

Okra is a popular Caribbean ingredient often referred to as 'ladies fingers'.

Cumin Kale

Ingredients:

- Serves 4
- Cooking Time: 20-25 mins

1 onion, finely sliced
2 garlic cloves, crushed
2 tsp olive oil or sunflower oil
250g/9oz kale, roughly chopped
2 tbsp water
1 tsp cumin powder
½ tsp ground coriander/cilantro
Lemon wedges to serve
Salt & pepper to taste

Method:

1. If your hot air fryer has a temperature control set it to 180C/350F.
2. Place the onions, garlic and oil in the hot air fryer and cook for 5 minutes.
3. Add the kale, water, cumin & coriander and cook for a further 15-20 minutes or until the kale is tender.
4. Season and serve with lemon wedges.

Remove any thick kale stalks, as they will be too tough for this dish.

Crushed Mango Potatoes

Ingredients:

500g/1lb 2oz baby new potatoes, halved
2 tsp olive oil or sunflower oil
1 tsp mango powder
½ tsp chilli powder
Salt & pepper to taste

Method:

1. If your hot air fryer has a temperature control set it to 180C/350F.
2. Place the new potatoes, oil, mango powder & chilli powder in the hot air fryer and cook for 25 minutes.
3. Take the potatoes out of the fryer and bash each one with a rolling pin.
4. Put back into the hot air fryer and cook for a further 15-20 minutes or until they are tender and cooked through.
5. Season and serve.

Don't smash up the potatoes too much. A single bash will be enough to give you the crushed texture you are looking for.

Mustard Cabbage

Ingredients:

- Serves 4
- Cooking Time: 20-25 mins

1 onion, sliced
2 tsp olive oil or sunflower oil
1 garlic clove, crushed
1 green pointed/Napa cabbage,
shredded
250g/9oz peas
2 tbsp water
2 tsp wholegrain mustard
Salt & pepper to taste

Method:

1. If your hot air fryer has a temperature control set it to 180C/350F.
2. Place the sliced onions, oil & garlic in the hot air fryer and cook for 5 minutes.
3. Add the cabbage, peas, water & mustard and cook for a further 15-20 minutes or until the cabbage & peas are tender.
4. Season and serve.

Add more mustard if you wish and season with lots of black pepper.

Sweet Coriander Carrots

- Serves 4
- Cooking Time: 10-15 mins

Ingredients:

400g/14oz carrots, cut into thin
batons
2 tsp olive oil or sunflower oil
1 tsp brown sugar
1 tsp ground coriander/cilantro
Salt & pepper to taste

Method:

1. If your hot air fryer has a temperature control set it to 180C/350F.
2. Place the carrots, oil, sugar and coriander in the hot air fryer and cook for 10-15 minutes or until the carrots are crispy and tender.
3. Season and serve immediately.

You may need to adjust your cooking time depending on how thinly or thickly you cut the carrots.

66

Asparagus & Sunblush Tomatoes

Ingredients:

400g/14oz asparagus tips
2 tsp olive oil or sunflower oil
200g/9oz sunblush/jarred sundried
tomatoes
1 tbsp balsamic vinegar
4 tbsp freshly chopped flat leaf
parsley
Salt & pepper to taste

- Serves 4
- Cooking Time: 10-14 mins

Method:

1. If your hot air fryer has a temperature control set it to 180C/350F.
2. Place the asparagus, oil, tomatoes & vinegar in the hot air fryer and cook for 10-14 minutes or until tender and cooked through.
3. Season and serve.

Jars of sunblush tomatoes are widely available at most supermarkets.

Dried Shrimp French Beans

Ingredients:

400g/14oz green beans
1 tbsp dried shrimp
1 tbsp soy sauce
1 tsp fish sauce
1 tbsp water
1 tbsp freshly grated ginger
2 tsp olive oil or sunflower oil
Salt & pepper to taste

Method:

1. If your hot air fryer has a temperature control set it to 180C/350F.
2. Place the French beans, dried shrimp, soy, fish sauce, water, ginger & oil in the hot air fryer and cook for 10-14 minutes or until tender and cooked through.

Dried shrimps are a potent Asian store cupboard ingredient, which pack a punch.

Celeriac Wedges

Ingredients:

2 large celeriac bulbs
1 tsp garlic powder
½ tsp salt
1 tsp mixed herbs
2 tsp olive oil or sunflower oil
Salt & pepper to taste

- Serves 4
- Cooking Time: 30-40 mins

Method:

1. If your hot air fryer has a temperature control set it to 180C/350F.
2. Peel the celeriac and cut each bulb into 10 wedges.
3. Pat dry the wedges and combine with the garlic, salt and mixed herbs.
4. Place in the hot air fryer with the oil and cook for 30-40 minutes or until the wedges are crisp on the outside & tender on the inside.
5. Season well and serve.

Try using sweet potato for this recipe too.

Stir Fried 'Colcannon'

Ingredients:

800g/1¾lb potatoes
2 garlic cloves, crushed
1 red chilli, finely chopped
1 tsp olive oil or sunflower oil
400g/14oz spring greens, shredded
½ tsp nutmeg
1 tbsp water
Salt & pepper to taste

Method:

1. If your hot air fryer has a temperature control set it to 180C/350F.
2. Peel the potatoes and cut into small 2cm square cubes. Give the cubes a rinse and dry them off really well with kitchen towel.
3. Place in the hot air fryer and cook for 20 minutes.
4. Add the rest of the ingredients and cook for an additional 10-15 minutes or until everything is cooked through and tender.
5. Season well and serve.

Colcannon is traditionally made using mashed potato, this is a hot air alternative.

Zucchini Crisps

Ingredients:

400g/14oz courgettes/zuchinni, very
finely sliced
2 tsp olive oil or sunflower oil
½ tsp salt
Salt & pepper to taste

- Serves 4
- Cooking Time: 10-15 mins

Method:

1. If your hot air fryer has a temperature control set it to 180C/350F.
2. Pat dry the courgette slices.
3. Add all the ingredients to the hot air fryer and cook for 10-15 minutes or until the 'crisps' are cooked and ready to eat.

Experiment with some other vegetables to make a range of tasty vegetable 'crisps'.

Spiced Shredded Chips

Ingredients:

4 soft flour tortilla wraps
1 tsp chilli powder
2 tsp olive oil or sunflower oil
½ tsp salt
Salt & pepper to taste

Method:

1. If your hot air fryer has a temperature control set it to 180C/350F.
2. Roll the tortilla wraps and cut into thin shredded slices.
3. Combine these shreds with the chilli powder, oil and salt and add to the hot air fryer.
4. Cook for 8-12 minutes or until the shredded tortilla slices are crispy and golden.
5. Season and serve.

Add more or less chilli to suit your own taste.

Italian Herb Fries

Ingredients:

800g/1¾lb potatoes
2 tsp olive oil or sunflower oil
½ tsp each dried thyme, rosemary &
garlic powder
Salt & pepper to taste

- Serves 4
- Cooking Time: 28-32 mins

Method:

1. If your hot air fryer has a temperature control set it to 180C/350F.
2. Leave the skin on the potatoes and cut into thin fries.
3. Give the fries a rinse and dry them off really well with kitchen towel.
4. Place the fries in the hot air fryer along with the dried herbs and oil.
5. Cook for 28-32 minutes or until the fries are crisp on the outside and tender on the inside.
6. Season and serve.

Rosemary & thyme are staples of Italian cooking. Try sage too if you have some to hand.

Sweet Potato Coconut Fries

Ingredients:

800g/1¾lb sweet potatoes
2 tsp coconut oil
Salt & pepper to taste

Method:

1. If your hot air fryer has a temperature control set it to 180C/350F.
2. Peel the sweet potatoes and cut into thin fries.
3. Give the fries a rinse and dry them off really well with kitchen towel.
4. Place the fries in the hot air fryer along with the coconut oil.
5. Cook for 20-25 minutes or until the fries are crisp on the outside and tender on the inside.
6. Season and serve.

A little cayenne pepper or paprika can also make a nice addition.

Sautéed Garlic Potatoes

Ingredients:

800g/1¾lb potatoes
2 tsp olive oil or sunflower oil
8 garlic cloves, crushed
1 tsp dried thyme
Salt & pepper to taste

• Serves 4
• Cooking Time: 35-40 mins

Method:

1. If your hot air fryer has a temperature control set it to 180C/350F.
2. Peel the potatoes and cut into small 2cm square cubes.
3. Give the cubes a rinse and dry them off really well with kitchen towel.
4. Place in the hot air fryer along with the garlic, thyme & oil and cook for 35-40 minutes or until the potato cubes are tender.
5. Season and serve.

Fresh thyme and/or rosemary works well for this simple recipe too.

Spicy Fried Lime Potatoes

Ingredients:

800g/1¾lb potatoes
2 tsp olive oil or sunflower oil
1 tsp crushed chilli flakes
Zest of one lime
Salt & pepper to taste

Method:

1. If your hot air fryer has a temperature control set it to 180C/350F.
2. Peel the potatoes and cut into small 2cm square cubes.
3. Give the cubes a good rinse and dry them off with kitchen towel.
4. Place in the hot air fryer along with the oil, chilli flakes & zest.
5. Cook for 35-40 minutes or until the potato cubes are crispy on the outside and tender on the inside.
6. Season and serve.

These potatoes are great served with low fat mayonnaise mixed with a squeeze of lime juice.

Parmesan Roastini

Ingredients:

800g/1¾lb premade gnocchi
2 tsp olive oil or sunflower oil
1 tbsp freshly grated Parmesan
Salt & pepper to taste

- Serves 4
- Cooking Time: 20-30 mins

Method:

1. If your hot air fryer has a temperature control set it to 180C/350F.
2. Place the gnocchi in the hot air fryer along with the oil.
3. Cook for 20-30 minutes or until the gnocchi is crispy on the outside and tender on the inside.
4. Season, sprinkle with the grated Parmesan cheese and serve.

Frying gnocchi is a relatively new idea, which has become increasingly popular thanks to celebrity chef Nigella Lawson.

Caribbean 'Crisps'

- Serves 4
- Cooking Time: 15-20 mins

Ingredients:

3 large sweet potatoes
2 tsp coconut oil
½ tsp paprika
Salt & pepper to taste

Method:

1. If your hot air fryer has a temperature control set it to 180C/350F.
2. Peel the potatoes and slice them into wafer-thin 'crisps' (some food processors have an attachment which will slice very thinly for you).
3. Place in the hot air fryer along with the paprika & oil and cook for 15-20 minutes or until they are cooked through and crispy.
4. Season and serve.

These crisps are very moreish and are great to have in bowls as party finger-food.

78

Greek Potatoes

Ingredients:

800g/1¾lb potatoes
2 tsp olive oil or sunflower oil
2 tsp dried oregano
Lemon wedges
Salt & pepper to taste

- Serves 4
- Cooking Time: 35-40 mins

Method:

1. If your hot air fryer has a temperature control set it to 180C/350F.
2. Peel the potatoes and cut into small 2cm square cubes.
3. Give the cubes a good rinse and dry them off well with kitchen towel.
4. Place in the hot air fryer along with the oregano & oil.
5. Cook for 35-40 minutes or until the potato cubes are crispy on the outside and tender on the inside.
6. Squeeze lemon juice over the fries, season and serve.

Season these potatoes with crushed sea salt and lots of freshly ground black pepper.

Sesame & Chilli Potatoes

- Serves 4
- Cooking Time: 35-40 mins

Ingredients:

800g/1¾lb potatoes
2 tsp sesame oil
½ tsp crushed chilli flakes
Salt & pepper to taste

Method:

1. If your hot air fryer has a temperature control set it to 180C/350F.
2. Peel the potatoes and cut into small 2cm square cubes.
3. Rinse, pat dry and put to one side.
4. Mix the potatoes and crushed chilli flakes together and place in the hot air fryer along with the oil.
5. Cook for 35-40 minutes or until the potato cubes are crispy on the outside and tender on the inside.
6. Season and serve.

You could also add some sesame seeds to these potatoes either during cooking or sprinkled over afterwards.

Balsamic Gnocchi

Ingredients:

800g/1¾lb premade gnochhi
2 tsp olive oil or sunflower oil
2 tsp balsamic vinegar
Salt & pepper to taste

- Serves 4
- Cooking Time: 20-30 mins

Method:

1. If your hot air fryer has a temperature control set it to 180C/350F.
2. Place the gnocchi in the hot air fryer along with the oil.
3. Cook for 10 minutes, add the balsamic vinegar and cook for a further 10-20 minutes or until the gnocchi is crispy on the outside and tender on the inside.
4. Season and serve.

Balsamic vinegar should add a nice glaze to the gnocchi, you could use a little runny honey towards the end of the cooking time if you prefer.

Garam Onions

Ingredients:

4 large onions, sliced
2 tsp garam masala
½ tsp salt
1 garlic clove, crushed
Salt & pepper to taste

Method:

1. If your hot air fryer has a temperature control set it to 180C/350F.
2. Add all the ingredients to the hot air fryer and cook for 15-20 minutes or until deliciously crisp and tender.
3. Season and serve.

Garam masala is a combined spice which is popular in Indian cooking. Balance its distinctive taste with salt.

CONVERSION CHART: DRY INGREDIENTS

Metric	Imperial
7g	¼ oz
15g	½ oz
20g	¾ oz
25g	1 oz
40g	1½oz
50g	2oz
60g	2½oz
75g	3oz
100g	3½oz
125g	4oz
140g	4½oz
150g	5oz
165g	5½oz
175g	6oz
200g	7oz
225g	8oz
250g	9oz
275g	10oz
300g	11oz
350g	12oz
375g	13oz
400g	14oz

Metric	Imperial
425g	15oz
450g	1lb
500g	1lb 2oz
550g	1¼lb
600g	1lb 5oz
650g	1lb 7oz
675g	1½lb
700g	1lb 9oz
750g	1lb 11oz
800g	1¾lb
900g	2lb
1kg	2¼lb
1.1kg	2½lb
1.25kg	2¾lb
1.35kg	3lb
1.5kg	3lb 6oz
1.8kg	4lb
2kg	4½lb
2.25kg	5lb
2.5kg	5½lb
2.75kg	6lb

CONVERSION CHART: LIQUID MEASURES

Metric	Imperial	US
25ml	1fl oz	
60ml	2fl oz	¼ cup
75ml	2½ fl oz	
100ml	3½fl oz	
120ml	4fl oz	½ cup
150ml	5fl oz	
175ml	6fl oz	
200ml	7fl oz	
250ml	8½ fl oz	1 cup
300ml	10½ fl oz	
360ml	12½ fl oz	
400ml	14fl oz	
450ml	15½ fl oz	
600ml	1 pint	
750ml	1¼ pint	3 cups
1 litre	1½ pints	4 cups

Other
COOKNATION
TITLES

If you enjoyed 'The Skinny Hot Air Fryer Cookbook' we'd really appreciate your feedback. Reviews help others decide if this is the right book for them so a moment of your time would be appreciated.

Thank you.

You may also be interested in other '**Skinny**' titles in the CookNation series. You can find all the following great titles by searching under '**CookNation**'.

The Skinny Slow Cooker Recipe Book

Delicious Recipes Under 300, 400 And 500 Calories.

Paperback / eBook

More Skinny Slow Cooker Recipes

75 More Delicious Recipes Under 300, 400 & 500 Calories.

Paperback / eBook

The Skinny Slow Cooker Curry Recipe Book

Low Calorie Curries From Around The World

Paperback / eBook

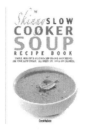

The Skinny Slow Cooker Soup Recipe Book

Simple, Healthy & Delicious Low Calorie Soup Recipes For Your Slow Cooker. All Under 100, 200 & 300 Calories.

Paperback / eBook

The Skinny Slow Cooker Vegetarian Recipe Book

40 Delicious Recipes Under 200, 300 And 400 Calories.

Paperback / eBook

The Skinny 5:2 Slow Cooker Recipe Book

Skinny Slow Cooker Recipe And Menu Ideas Under 100, 200, 300 & 400 Calories For Your 5:2 Diet.

Paperback / eBook

The Skinny 5:2 Curry Recipe Book

Spice Up Your Fast Days With Simple Low Calorie Curries, Snacks, Soups, Salads & Sides Under 200, 300 & 400 Calories

Paperback / eBook

The Skinny Halogen Oven Family Favourites Recipe Book

Healthy, Low Calorie Family Meal-Time Halogen Oven Recipes Under 300, 400 and 500 Calories

Paperback / eBook

Skinny Halogen Oven Cooking For One

Single Serving, Healthy, Low Calorie Halogen Oven Recipes Under 200, 300 and 400 Calories

Paperback / eBook

Skinny Winter Warmers Recipe Book

Soups, Stews, Casseroles & One Pot Meals Under 300, 400 & 500 Calories.

Paperback / eBook

The Skinny Soup Maker Recipe Book

Delicious Low Calorie, Healthy and Simple Soup Recipes Under 100, 200 and 300 Calories. Perfect For Any Diet and Weight Loss Plan.

Paperback / eBook

The Skinny Bread Machine Recipe Book

70 Simple, Lower Calorie, Healthy Breads...Baked To Perfection In Your Bread Maker.

Paperback / eBook

The Skinny Indian Takeaway Recipe Book

Authentic British Indian Restaurant Dishes Under 300, 400 And 500 Calories. The Secret To Low Calorie Indian Takeaway Food At Home

Paperback / eBook

The Skinny Juice Diet Recipe Book

5lbs, 5 Days. The Ultimate Kick-Start Diet and Detox Plan to Lose Weight & Feel Great!

Paperback / eBook

The Skinny 5:2 Diet Recipe Book Collection

All The 5:2 Fast Diet Recipes You'll Ever Need. All Under 100, 200, 300, 400 And 500 Calories

Available only on eBook

eBook

The Skinny 5:2 Fast Diet Meals For One

Single Serving Fast Day Recipes & Snacks Under 100, 200 & 300 Calories

Paperback / eBook

The Skinny 5:2 Fast Diet Vegetarian Meals For One

Single Serving Fast Day Recipes & Snacks Under 100, 200 & 300 Calories

Paperback / eBook

The Skinny 5:2 Fast Diet Family Favourites Recipe Book

Eat With All The Family On Your Diet Fasting Days

Paperback / eBook

The Skinny 5:2 Fast Diet Family Favorites Recipe Book *U.S.A. EDITION*

Dine With All The Family On Your Diet Fasting Days

Available only on eBook

The Skinny 5:2 Diet Chicken Dishes Recipe Book

Delicious Low Calorie Chicken Dishes Under 300, 400 & 500 Calories

Paperback / eBook

89

The Skinny 5:2 Bikini Diet Recipe Book

Recipes & Meal Planners Under 100, 200 & 300 Calories. Get Ready For Summer & Lose Weight...FAST!

Paperback / eBook

The Paleo Diet For Beginners Slow Cooker Recipe Book

Gluten Free, Everyday Essential Slow Cooker Paleo Recipes For Beginners

Available only on eBook

eBook

The Paleo Diet For Beginners Meals For One

The Ultimate Paleo Single Serving Cookbook

Paperback / eBook

The Paleo Diet For Beginners Holidays

Thanksgiving, Christmas & New Year Paleo Friendly Recipes

Available only on eBook

eBook

The Healthy Kids Smoothie Book

40 Delicious Goodness In A Glass Recipes for Happy Kids.

Available only on eBook

eBook

The Skinny Slow Cooker Summer Recipe Book

Fresh & Seasonal Summer Recipes For Your Slow Cooker. All Under 300, 400 And 500 Calories.

Paperback / eBook

The Skinny ActiFry Cookbook

Guilt-free and Delicious ActiFry Recipe Ideas: Discover The Healthier Way to Fry!

Paperback / eBook

The Skinny 15 Minute Meals Recipe Book

Delicious, Nutritious & Super-Fast Meals in 15 Minutes Or Less. All Under 300, 400 & 500 Calories.

Paperback / eBook

The Skinny Mediterranean Recipe Book

Simple, Healthy & Delicious Low Calorie Mediterranean Diet Dishes. All Under 200, 300 & 400 Calories.

Paperback / eBook

The Skinny Hot Air Fryer Cookbook

Delicious & Simple Meals For Your Hot Air Fryer: Discover The Healthier Way To Fry.

Paperback / eBook

The Skinny Ice Cream Maker

Delicious Lower Fat, Lower Calorie Ice Cream, Frozen Yogurt & Sorbet Recipes For Your Ice Cream Maker

Paperback / eBook

The Skinny Low Calorie Recipe Book

Great Tasting, Simple & Healthy Meals Under 300, 400 & 500 Calories. Perfect For Any Calorie Controlled Diet.

Paperback / eBook

The Skinny Takeaway Recipe Book

Healthier Versions Of Your Fast Food Favourites: Chinese, Indian, Pizza, Burgers, Southern Style Chicken, Mexican & More. All Under 300, 400 & 500 Calories

Paperback / eBook

The Skinny Nutribullet Recipe Book

80+ Delicious & Nutritious Healthy Smoothie Recipes. Burn Fat, Lose Weight and Feel Great!

Paperback / eBook

The Skinny Nutribullet Soup Recipe Book

Delicious, Quick & Easy, Single Serving Soups & Pasta Sauces For Your Nutribullet. All Under 100, 200, 300 & 400 Calories.

Paperback / eBook

Made in the USA
Middletown, DE
21 December 2016